REACHING FOR THE STARS

MACAULAY CULKIN
Child Movie Star

Written by Rosemary Wallner

Published by Abdo & Daughters, 4940 Viking Drive Suite 622, Edina, Minnesota 55435.

Library bound edition distributed by Rockbottom Books, Pentagon Tower, P.O. Box 36036, Minneapolis, Minnesota 55435.

ISBN: 1-56239-227-1

Cover photo: AP Photo Color
Inside photos: Archive Photos/Fotos International: 5,8,9,29
                AP/World Wide Photos: 14,16,21,24,25,31

Edited by Julie Berg

LIBRARY OF CONGRESS CATALOGING-IN-PUBLICATION DATA
Wallner, Rosemary, 1964-
    Macaulay Culkin / written by Rosemary Wallner. -- 1st ed.
      p. cm. -- (Reaching for the Stars)
    Includes bibliographical references and index.
    Summary: Presents the life of the young actor who achieved stardom in the movie "Home Alone."
    ISBN 1-56239-227-1
    1. Culkin, Macaulay, 1980-   -- Juvenile literature. 2. Motion picture actors and actresses -- United States -- Biography -- Juvenile literature. [1. Culkin, Macaulay, 1980- . 2. Actors and actresses.] I. Title. II. Series.
    PN2287.C688W35   1993
    791.43'028'092--dc20
    [B]   93-19061
                                  CIP
                          AC MN

TABLE OF CONTENTS

THE SCREAM

When you think of Macaulay Culkin, what do you think of? Thousands of moviegoers think of Mac's famous scream. He slaps his hands to his cheeks and bulges his eyes. With his mouth wide open, Macaulay lets out a screaming, "AAAAAAH!!!!"

That scream was made famous in the 1990 hit movie *Home Alone*. In the movie, Macaulay's character puts on his father's after-shave lotion. He puts a little on his hands and slaps his hands to his face. The stinging feeling makes him yell, "AAAAAAH!!!!"

Home Alone was a success. It became the third highest grossing film of all time. Only 1977's *Star Wars* and 1982's *E.T.* have made more money.

On the movie set, Mac (as his friends call him) can be a trouble-maker. He has booby-trapped doors and stolen the director's microphone. Off the set, he has thrown water balloons out of hotel windows with his friend Michael Jackson.

Despite his young age, Mac has continued his acting career. He played Kevin McCallister in *Home Alone* and *Home Alone 2: Lost in New York*. He has even acted in more serious roles.

Because of these other roles, Mac's father advised him to stop screaming for reporters. As Mac told one reporter, "I'm trying to get a different character, you know?"

Director Chris Columbus on the set of "Home Alone" with star Macaulay Culkin. Macaulay played the part of Kevin McCallister who has to defend his house against a pair of bumbling burglars.

FAMILY LIFE

Macaulay Culkin was born on August 26, 1980. Mac's parents named their third child after Thomas Babbington Macaulay, a British historian.

Mac's father, Kit Culkin, was an actor. He began appearing in commercials when he was 10 years old. By the 1970s, however, Kit's acting career had almost ended and he was living out of a tent in California. In 1974, Kit decided to travel back to New York. On his way through Wyoming, he met his future wife Pat.

Mac's mother, Pat, grew up in a large family in New England, North Dakota. When she met Kit, she was 19 years old and worked at a construction site. She was directing traffic around the site when Kit pulled up. The two started talking and found out they had much in common. Eventually, Pat decided to head to New York with Kit and get married.

Once in New York, Kit continued to look for acting jobs. Pat stayed home and took care of their family. By the late 1980s, the Culkins had seven children. They had five sons: Shane, Mac, Kieran, Christian, and Rory. And they had two daughters: Dakata and Quinn.

The Culkins lived in a four-room apartment on Manhattan's Upper East side. Mac and his brothers and sisters shared one bedroom. Each child had a bed and a shelf for toys. Kit Culkin worked as a sacristan at nearby St. Joseph's church. He looked after the ceremonial cups and robes. In exchange, the Catholic school reduced the tuition so that Mac, his brothers, and older sister could attend the school. Pat Culkin answered phones for an answering service.

The Culkin's life changed in 1984. That year, four-year-old Mac appeared in a local show called "Bach Babies," and his parents saw the first signs of Mac's acting talent. His father remembered that Mac was not self-conscious in front of the audience. He didn't even look for his parents. He did a little dance step and the audience laughed. Kit knew that his son had a special charm.

EARLY ACTING JOBS

Although Mac had acting talent, his older brother, Shane, was the first to begin an acting career. Susan Selig, a friend of Mac's father, worked at the Ensemble Studio Theater in New York. She suggested that Shane try out for a part in a play. Shane got the part and the whole family met the director Billy Hopkins.

In 1986, Hopkins was directing another play and he needed to cast a young boy. He thought that Shane was too old for the part, but Hopkins remembered that Shane had some younger brothers. He contacted the Culkins and told them about his new play. Kit and Pat decided to take six-year-old Mac to the audition.

When Hopkins met Mac, he noticed a twinkle in the young boy's eye and a mischievous grin. He knew that Mac would be right for the part. Mac learned his lines by repeating them over and

Macaulay Culkin with star John Candy in the hit movie "Uncle Buck".

Macaulay played John Candy's nephew, Miles, in "Uncle Buck". After playing this role, Mac's acting career really took off.

over again. When the play, *After School Special*, opened in 1987, the critics loved Mac. *The New York Times* and the *New Yorker* praised the play and Mac's acting.

With his success in the play, Mac found a children's talent agency to represent him. By the time he was seven-years-old, he had been offered a part in the movie *Rocket Gibraltar*.

The 1987 movie *Rocket Gibraltar* starred Burt Lancaster as an aging grandfather. Mac played one of his grandsons. During filming, Mac learned much about acting and listening to directors. On one of the first days of filming, the director told Mac to ride a bike down the street. Mac got on the bike and rode past the cameras. The director yelled, "Cut." But Mac didn't know that "Cut" meant "Stop" so he kept pedaling. A production assistant had to flag him down.

Shortly after *Rocket Gibraltar*, Mac got a small part in *See You in the Morning*. That film starred Jeff Bridges and Farrah Fawcett; Mac played the son. Both of these films helped start his acting career. His third film, *Uncle Buck*, brought him a little closer to stardom.

Uncle Buck starred John Candy. The movie was about an out-of-work man who baby-sits his brother's children. Mac played Candy's nephew, Miles Russell, who is suspicious of his large, messy uncle. In one scene, Miles asks his uncle all sorts of questions.

In another scene, Miles guards his family's home when his uncle leaves. He sits behind the mail slot in the door waiting to defend his home.

Mac was beginning to enjoy his acting jobs. He liked pretending he was someone else. He didn't know that within a year his small acting jobs would lead to super stardom.

HOME ALONE

Writer and director John Hughes had created many movies—including *Uncle Buck*. As he worked on that movie, one scene kept staying in his mind. He kept thinking about the part when Miles guards his home by looking out the front door's mail slot. Hughes wondered if he could write another movie where a child protects his home.

After completing *Uncle Buck*, Hughes and his family decided to take a vacation. Hughes made a list of everything he wanted to take. "I better not forget my kids," he thought to himself. Then he thought, "What would happen if I did forget them?" Hughes took a break from packing and wrote eight pages of notes. Those notes developed into the screenplay for *Home Alone*.

Hughes's story was about Kevin McCallister, the youngest son in a large family. On the night before his family leaves for Paris, Kevin gets mad at his parents and is sent to bed early. He angrily tells his mom, "I don't want to see you ever again for the rest of my whole life!" The next morning, in the rush to get to the airport, his family forgets him at home.

When Kevin wakes up, he finds everyone gone and thinks his wish has come true. He is happy until he realizes that two burglars have planned to rob his home. At the movie's high point, Kevin booby-traps his home and foils the burglars.

Hughes and director Chris Columbus knew that they had to find the right actor to play the part of Kevin. Both were looking for a regular kid to play the part. They didn't want a young actor who had forgotten how to be a kid. Hughes remembered working with Mac in *Uncle Buck* and thought he should star in his new movie. But Columbus also had to approve of Mac.

Columbus auditioned hundreds of boys. When he met Mac, he thought that the young actor was just who he had been looking for. "I knew he'd be perfect," remembered Columbus. The director saw that not only did Mac have a special talent, but he also still acted like a kid.

Home Alone was filmed in a suburb of Chicago. Whenever the days of filming got too long, Columbus found fun ways to keep Mac interested. After each day of rehearsal, he rewarded Mac with a Nintendo game.

Mac was busy with rehearsals, but he also found time to set up pranks. He used string in elaborate and strange ways. He booby-trapped doors with buckets of confetti. Before long, the cast and crew members learned to watch out for Mac. No one wanted to be his next victim.

Twentieth Century Fox released *Home Alone* on November 16, 1990. They waited to see what audiences would think of the comedy.

They didn't have to wait long, however. The movie became an instant hit—everyone seemed to love it. Newspapers called it the year's funniest slapstick mayhem.

Hughes believes that kids like the movie because Kevin doesn't use superhuman power to guard his home. He outwits the burglars using plain, household items. Mac's running around and his famous scream also attracted viewers. "This kid gets bigger on the screen," said Hughes about Mac. "I don't know why."

The movie had cost $15 million to make. For two months, it remained on the top of the hit list. By December 1991, one year after its release, *Home Alone* had earned $507 million. It also had made Macaulay Culkin a movie star.

AFTER HOME ALONE:
SUCCESS AND FAME

Everyone was amazed at *Home Alone's* success. "*Home Alone* was a perfect idea with the perfect person—that's what creates movie stars," said Tom Jacobson, head of production for the movie.

Soon after the movie's release, stores began to sell Kevin McCallister dolls. When someone pressed a button in the doll's back, its arms went up and it screamed, "AAAAAAH!!!!" *Home Alone* video games, T-shirts, and trading cards also appeared.

Macaulay Culkin, star of the hit movie "Home Alone", clowns around with his co-star Joe Pesci at a production party.

What did Mac feel about all of this sudden fame? He just accepted it. When fans told him how much they loved the movie and how much they love him, he just smiled.

Many people wanted to interview Mac and ask him all sorts of questions. In one interview, Kevin got bored and answered questions as simply as he could. When the reporter asked Mac what it was like to be a star, Mac said, "It's okay." When she asked if Mac liked riding in fancy cars, he said, "It's okay." When she asked if it was fun giving autographs, he said, "It's okay."

Another reporter asked Mac if any of his friends were excited about the movie. He replied that it was no big deal. "They already knew about *Home Alone* before it came out," he shrugged.

BEHIND THE SCENES

As Fox Studios enjoyed the success of *Home Alone,* Mac found that his life at home was changing. Shortly after the movie came out, Mac's parents separated. They worked out their problems, though, and got back together. Mac's family then decided they needed a larger place to live. They moved into a five-bedroom apartment in New York.

Another change happened when both of his parents quit their jobs to manage their son's career. But Mac doesn't mind this arrangement. He likes having his parents around and trusts their judgment. "My parents read a script and tell me what I'm going to do in the movie," he explained.

Macaulay lives with his family in a five-bedroom apartment in New York City. The background of this photo shows Central Park where Macaulay lives.

Whenever reporters ask Mac how much money he makes, Mac replies, "I don't know." As his managers, Mac's parents don't want him to know how much he earns.

They don't want him to become spoiled, so they put all his money into a trust fund. When he is older, he will use that money to go to college. Mac's parents usually reward Mac with a trip to a toy store. To earn his $5 a week allowance, Mac has to make his bed and clean his room.

After *Home Alone,* Mac's parents continued to look for acting projects for him. A year after *Home Alone,* Mac starred in his own Saturday morning cartoon. "Wishkid Starring Macaulay Culkin" began in November 1991. Nicholas McClary, a cartoon character, was drawn to look like Mac. Each week, a magical star granted Nicholas one wish. Mac appeared at the beginning of each show to tell the audience about the episode.

For appearing in only 13 episodes, Mac earned $500,000. But the cartoon show didn't last too long, and Mac continued with other projects. In December 1991, he appeared in commercials for Apple computers and Dr. Pepper. Mac also appeared in the horror movie *Jacob's Ladder.* He played the deceased son of a man who has nightmares of the boy. Mac and his brother Kieran also had a small role in *Only the Lonely,* another John Candy movie.

MY GIRL

In 1990, David Friendly saw a preview of *Home Alone;* he liked the way Mac acted. He was going to produce *My Girl* and asked

Mac to play the part of a character named Thomas J. "He had more presence than any child actor I can remember," said Friendly.

At the audition, Friendly recalled that Mac had a mischievous streak. Every time the director asked him to do something, Mac slyly smiled and asked, "Director, may I?" But afterwards, Mac shook hands with everyone in the room. "He acted like a real professional," said Friendly.

My Girl is the story of Veda, a lonely girl being raised by her father. Mac played the girl's friend. Mac's parents approved of the movie because Mac's role was small. They wanted to protect their son from the publicity he had endured during *Home Alone*.

The film's star was Anna Chlumsky, a 10-year-old actress from Chicago. She had acted in plays, including *Annie,* but *My Girl* was her first screen role. Mac and Anna met before filming started. They got to know each other by biking around the set and catching bugs.

"She is fun to work with because she's a kid," said Mac about Anna. "And kids relate to kids better than they relate to adults."

"Mac's an easy person to get along with," revealed Anna. "But he's a mean teaser."

Once the two actors got to know each other, filming began. Howard Zieff, the director, said Mac listened better than any other actor he had worked with. "I just pretend I'm a character," said Mac. "I like pretending. Acting is simple."

During one scene, Thomas J. and Veda kiss. Mac and Anna were a little nervous about their first on-screen kiss. It took a few tries to get the kiss just right. "We did eight takes of kisses on the count of 'One, two, three, kiss,' " remembered Zieff.

When Mac wasn't filming, he was usually signing autographs. Each day, a large crowd gathered on the street where the cast and crew worked. One day, a group of boys on bicycles rode up and asked Mac to autograph their denim jackets. Mac grabbed a pen and wrote out his first name. For his last name, he only wrote "Cul" and a long line. "It looks cool and saves time," Mac later told a reporter.

When *My Girl* was finished, Columbia Pictures wanted people to see the film so they put ads in newspapers saying that the movie starred Macaulay Culkin. Mac's parents were not happy because suddenly reporters were everywhere again, trying to talk to their son. After awhile, moviegoers realized that Anna was the real star of the movie, but Mac continued to get more and more attention.

SCHOOLWORK ON MOVIE SETS

Mac attends the Professional Children's School in New York. During filming, however, he relies on tutors to help him keep up with his classmates.

Jennifer While was Mac's tutor on the set of *Home Alone*. For five months, she worked with Mac. His teachers in New York shipped lesson plans to Chicago.

The teachers prepared classes on religion, history, math, science, and English. His courses were the same as many other grammar school students.

Mac's tutor remembered that English was one subject Mac did not like. "Mac would whine, 'Do we have to write out the answers?' " said Jennifer While. "We ended up doing a lot of reading out loud."

On the set of *My Girl,* Leah Girolami tutored both Anna and Mac. For three hours a day, Girolami taught the young stars. Sometimes, she coached Anna and Mac during spelling bees. Although Mac did not like spelling, he always tried to beat Anna. Usually, though, Girolami did not teach Anna and Mac at the same time because they goofed off too much.

At the time, Anna and Mac were both in sixth grade. Their teachers sent lessons to the movie set in Florida. "But," said Girolami, "it's not like a real school. We were in a camper with no blackboard."

Although Mac learned the same subjects as his friends back home, school on the set is different. He does not have any homework. "He has to study his lines at night," explained Girolami. When it comes to taking a test, Mac sits down with his teacher and answers each question verbally. While he is on the set, he does not get any grades. For field trips, Mac's tutors take him to local museums. When he was filming *Home Alone,* his tutor took him to Chicago's Museum of Science and Industry.

Macaulay has to do school work like every other grammar school student does. He has a tutor and studies on the set of his movies.

Going to school on a movie set is hard. On the set, Mac has to worry about memorizing lines. He has to remember where to sit, stand, and walk. Sometimes, Mac had to go to school after working all day. One night, Mac was supposed to read a book about the Alamo, but he was so tired that Girolami ended up reading the whole book. "I left knowing more about the Alamo than he did," she said.

On another weary night, Girolami told Mac to sit down and watch the movie *The Ten Commandments*. She used the movie as an easy religion class.

"He's very smart," said Girolami about Mac. "He just loves math, especially when the problem is about money. I would say, 'Mac, if I gave you so much money, how would you invest it?' "

Whenever the pressures of acting got too much for Mac, he knew he could talk to Girolami. One day during filming, Mac was having a hard time with his lines. As he was doing his school-work, he almost started to cry. "I sat him down and told him that there's a lot of pressure on you," said Girolami. "There's a lot of pressure in this business."

HOME ALONE 2: Lost in New York

After *Home Alone* became a success, John Hughes wanted to make another movie about Kevin McCallister. Hughes thought about other adventures for the young boy. He thought it would be funny if Kevin lost his family at an airport and boarded a plane for New York.

Kevin would use his mom's credit cards to check into a hotel. His troubles would begin when he meets the two burglars from the first movie.

Hughes wanted *Home Alone 2: Lost in New York* to be as crazy and wacky as the first *Home Alone.* And he wanted Mac to star in this movie, too.

Hughes told Mac that he would be acting in *Home Alone 2,* but he did not tell Mac what the movie was about. He wanted the plot to be a secret. As soon as reporters heard about the new movie, they pestered Mac with questions about it. Mac truthfully answered that he did not know anything about the story line.

Chris Columbus, *Home Alone's* director, also worked on *Home Alone 2.* But filming in New York was much different from filming in a suburb of Chicago. In the movie, Kevin meets Pigeon Lady, Brenda Fricker. For 12 weeks, Columbus trained 350 pigeons to sit around the pigeon lady. He also had to shoot scenes on busy streets and in a busy airport. He had to keep the camera on Mac and the other actors while keeping out bystanders.

During filming, Mac had his own problems. When he was filming *Home Alone,* he was an unknown actor. People did not notice him. But things had changed and Mac was now a movie star. During *Home Alone 2,* a crowd stood outside his trailer all day. The fans screamed every time they saw him. The crowd upset Catherine O'Hara, who played the mother in *Home Alone.*

Macaulay Culkin gestures as he laughs with "Saturday Night Live" comedian Rob Schneider.

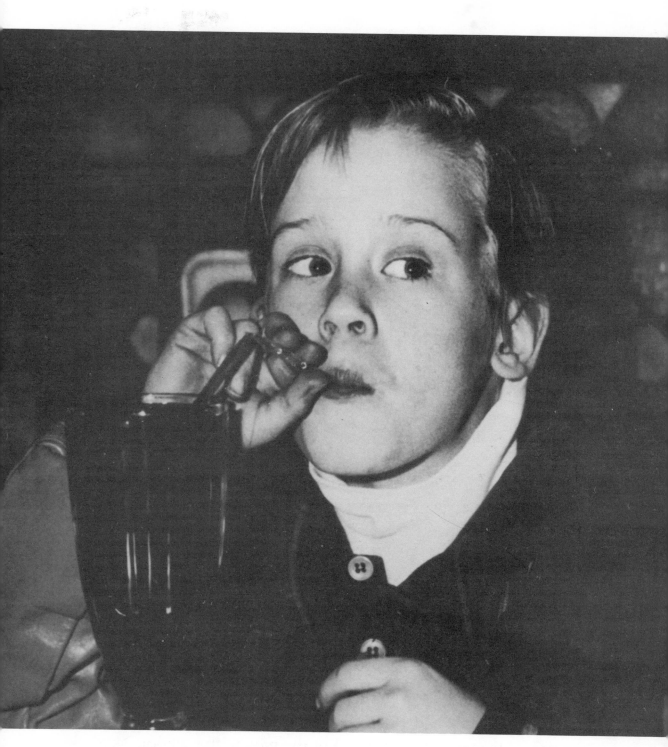

Macaulay, resting after a hard day on the set of one of his movies.

She told Mac to stick his head out and say, "What do you want? I'm only a child!"

Home Alone 2 was released in November 1992. The movie was not as successful as the first one, but Mac's fans thoroughly enjoyed it.

MORE ACTING AND MEETING MICHAEL JACKSON

After *Home Alone 2,* Mac's parents thought that he should act in a play. In a play, Mac would act in front of an audience, not in front of cameras. Mac agreed and soon got a part in *Sam I Am.* The play's director was Billy Hopkins, the same man who had directed Mac in his first play.

Although he was acting in front of an audience, Mac was still his mischievous self. During one scene, a character scolds Mac. Without telling anyone, Mac slapped his hands to his face and hollered, "AAAAAAH!!!!" The audience roared with laughter. Mac worked hard not to smile. Hopkins told Mac to keep his scream in the scene.

In 1992, the New York City Ballet decided to make a movie of the ballet "The Nutcracker." Dancers from the American School of Ballet would perform for movie cameras. Mac had studied at the school in 1988 and 1989. While he was there, he had played the part of the naughty brother. For the movie, the school asked Mac to play the part of the prince.

"The Nutcracker" is about a young girl who receives a nutcracker doll. Late one night, the nutcracker turns into a prince. In his pink satin suit, Mac danced and rehearsed with the rest of the dancers.

Whether he is acting on stage or in a movie, Mac said that there is one part of acting he does not like. The toughest part, he said, is being away from his family. He also gets tired of reporters asking him questions. Because reporters called his home all the time, his parents kept changing their phone number so people would leave them alone. One time, Mac had to call a friend because he could not remember his newest phone number.

Reporters sometimes ask Mac if he has met anyone interesting in show business. "Not really," Mac replies. One person Mac could mention, though, is his friend Michael Jackson.

Superstar singer Michael Jackson is over thirty years old. Mac is not quite a teenager. The age difference doesn't matter; the two have fun together. They have played pool at Neverland, Michael's ranch in California. They have even put on disguises and shopped together. (Michael put on a false nose and buck teeth. Mac put on sunglasses and a hat.) Michael also asked Mac to appear in the opening scenes of his "Black or White" video.

Michael has given Mac all sorts of toys and games. He gave Mac a 5-foot-long car and a full-size video arcade game. In the Culkin's small living room sits a huge entertainment center that Michael gave the family.

Mac's mom says that Michael likes to visit the Culkins because they do not care that he is famous. "My kids have a good time," said Pat Culkin. "Michael really is a good guy."

A REGULAR KID

Despite all of his fame, Mac still thinks of himself as a regular kid. He likes to put on baggy jeans, a Chicago Bears T-shirt, and high-top sneakers. Because he goes to award ceremonies, he has had to wear a tuxedo once in awhile. But he doesn't like it. "Boy, that suffocates me," he complained.

Mac likes to skateboard and watch wrestling on TV. In fact, Mac sometimes watches too much TV. "I have a TV in my room and a lock on my door," said Mac. "So my parents can't limit how much I watch."

Mac also likes to go bowling. On one Saturday afternoon, he went to a local bowling alley with his mother and his brother and sister. The bowling alley was full of families. But no one recognized Mac because he had grown his hair and it was longer than in *Home Alone 2*.

Since Mac has become famous, his brothers and sisters have begun to act more, also. Mac's brother Kieran had a small part in *Home Alone*. He played the young, bed-wetting cousin. His sister Quinn was the voice of one of the characters on the cartoon "Wishkid." His brother Shane has acted in many plays.

Chris Columbus, director of "Home Alone", thinks Macaulay could keep acting if he doesn't get bored with it. He also thinks Mac will maybe become a director.

What acting jobs are in Mac's future? His father wants Mac to play an evil cousin in a movie called *The Good Son.* Mac is also thinking about playing Richie Rich, a comic book character. But, said Mac, "I don't think about stuff that far ahead."

Director Chris Columbus thinks that Mac could keep acting if he doesn't get bored with it. There might, however, be other jobs for Mac. "Mac was always interested in the cameras," said Columbus. "Who knows, maybe he'll be a director one day."

When a reporter asked Mac if he planned to keep acting, Mac said, "Pretty much so." Then, as usual, Mac became bored with the interview. But the reporter wanted to ask him one more question. He asked if Mac would want to do something else when he got older. Mac paused. He answered simply, "Perhaps."

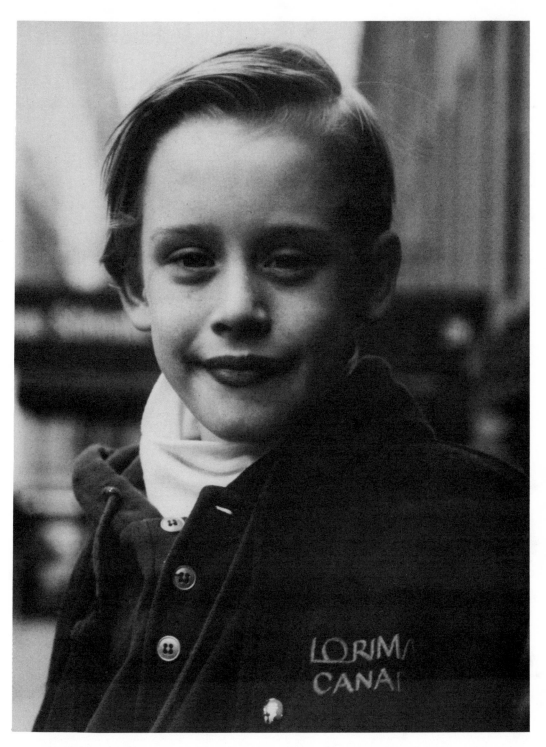

Macaulay Culkin, star of the hit movies "Home Alone" and "Home Alone 2".

MACAULAY CULKIN'S ADDRESS

You can write to Macaulay Culkin at:

Macaulay Culkin
ICM Agency
40 West 57th Street
New York, NY 10019

If you want to receive a reply, enclose a self-addressed stamped envelope.